靜思精舍惜物造福的智慧故事❷

行願
香積飯的故事

總策劃 / 靜思書軒

The Wisdom of Cherishing and Sowing Blessings
at the Jing Si Abode (2)
Vow to Action: The Story of Jing Si Instant Rice

「媽媽，我好餓喔！」小願撒嬌說。

「你要不要試試看『香積飯』？」媽媽從櫃子裡拿出一包香積飯。

「『香積飯』？聽起來香噴噴的，可是飯還要用電鍋煮，我現在好餓喔⋯⋯」。媽媽露出一個神祕笑容說：「不用等太久，你先回房間休息一下。」

"Mom, I'm hungry," Xiao-Yuan whined.

"Well, do you want to try this Jing Si Instant Rice?" Xiao-Yuan's mother brought out a packet of rice from the cupboard.

"Jing Si Instant Rice? That sounds nice! But you still need to cook the rice,
and I'm hungry now..."

Xiao-Yan's mother smiled mysteriously, and said, "It won't take long. Why don't you wait in your room?"

一會兒，「嗶！嗶！嗶」定時器響了，媽媽從廚房端出一碗飯和小願喜歡的小菜，「小願，出來吃香積飯囉！」小願邊吃邊跟媽媽比愛心。

小願說：「媽媽，我們下星期要交一篇作文，題目是『一頓飯』，我要來寫『香積飯』的故事，我們一起去靜思精舍採訪。」

Soon, the timer beeped loudly. "Beep! Beep! Beep!"

Xiao-Yuan's mother brought a bowl of rice from the kitchen, alongside some of Xiao-Yuan's favorite side dishes. "Xiao-Yuan, the Jing Si Rice is ready!" Xiao-Yuan made hearts with her fingers as she ate her rice.

"Mom, we need to write an essay next week, and the title is 'A Meal,'" Xiao-Yuan said, "And I want to write about the Jing Si Instant Rice. Can we visit the Jing Si Abode together so I can interview the Dharma Masters and learn how the rice is made?"

「師父您好，我是小願。『香積飯』這麼好吃又這麼方便，您是怎麼發明出來的？」小願問。

德晗師父笑咪咪說：「小願好，歡迎回家！香積飯不是我發明的，我只是依循前人的腳步，慢慢磨練出來的。」

" Hello, Dharma Master, I am Xiao-Yuan! The Jing Si Instant Rice is delicious, but it's also so easy to cook. How did you create it?" Xiao-Yuan asked.

Dharma Master De Han said with a smile, "Hello! Welcome! Xiao-Yuan. I did not invent the Jing Si Instant Rice. Instead, I merely gradually developed it by following in the footsteps of those who came before me."

「我嘗試許多不同的做法，研發期間，證嚴上人提醒我要做紀錄，這樣才知道米和水的比例。於是我先從煮飯開始研究，我一邊實驗一邊記錄，幾乎把花蓮的米種都買回來實驗，才慢慢研發成功。」德晗師父娓娓道來。

"I tried so many different methods! Dharma Master Cheng Yen also reminded me to make careful records during the development process. This way, I would be able to find the right ratio for the rice and the water. So I did many experiments, starting with cooking the rice, and recording my findings each time. I might have tested every type of rice grown in Hualien! But, in the end, I managed to succeed," Dharma Master De Han said.

「少量的米乾燥成功後，接下來要大量生產。可是，一樣的米種，一樣的比例，一樣的步驟，換了大臺的新機器，之前的努力又被打回原形！我體悟到原來研發香積飯的過程就是一種修行，慢慢放下焦躁的心，靜下心就有辦法。」

"After we managed to make a small amount of dried rice, the next thing to figure out was how to make lots of it. But we found that the same methods and ratios used on the same rice wouldn't work when we tried using a larger machine! All of our efforts had been for nothing! It was then that I understood that making Jing Si Instant Rice is a lot like spiritual cultivation; we have to do it with patience, without rushing."

「於是，我開始天馬行空的做各種實驗，什麼奇怪的想法都不放過。例如：用梳子梳飯、用噴槍噴飯，用各種角度思考問題。一個月後，發現問題出在機器，終於知道哪裡打結了。後來，我將機器調整之後，21公斤的白米大軍終於可以大量生產出香積飯了。」

"So I started doing all sorts of strange experiments. Nothing was too strange for me to try! I tried combing the rice with combs, and I even tried using a blowtorch! I examined the problem from every angle! Eventually, after a month, I realized that the problem was with the machine, so this meant I could make the right adjustments to it. The machine could now cook 21 kilograms of rice at a time to make lots of Jing Si Instant Rice!"

「我把香積飯寄給幾位國際人道救援會的實業家品嘗，他們非常驚豔，認為香積飯的味道不輸給日本乾燥飯，於是想要來參觀研發室。我的研發室就是穀粉間的水槽，後來換到桂花樹下，再來就是樓梯板架上木板，只要可以洗米、淘米、把鍋子架起來煮飯的地方，都可以是研發室。」

"I sent the rice to some business owners who were members of the Tzu Chi International Humanitarian Aid Association, and they were pleasantly surprised by it. They said it tasted just as good as the instant rice made in Japan! They asked me if they could visit the lab where we made the rice. But my lab was simply the sink in the workshop at the Jing Si Abode, then under the osmanthus tree, and then a wooden plank on the stairs. As long as there was somewhere I could wash the rice, portion it out, and cook it in a pot, I would use it as a lab."

「請問師父，香積飯的名字是怎麼來的呢？」小願誠心的問。

「『香積』一詞來自佛經，『香』是芬芳馥馨，『積』是因緣積聚。來自靜思精舍的乾燥飯，更是深受佛陀妙法的啟迪，以香積飯為名，再恰好不過。」德晗師父說。

"Dharma Master, how did you come up with the name of the Jing Si Instant Rice?" Xiao-Yuan asked curiously.

"Jing Si Instant Rice is called xiang ji fan in Chinese, where 'xiang ji' is a phrase from the Buddhist sutras. 'Xiang' means aromatic, like the smell of flowers, while 'ji' means to accumulate good karma. This is why we felt that 'xiang ji' would be a good name for the Jing Si Instant Rice, a type of rice that has been inspired by Buddhist philosophy and a desire to do good," Dharma Master De Han replied.

「香積飯有四個特色，第一個，急難救援，熱食送暖。在災區裡能夠快速提供大家溫飽，並顧及衛生和方便，除了災民，賑災的工作人員也需要好好吃飯和休息，營養均衡的香積飯正好可以幫助大家補充體力。」

"The Jing Si Instant Rice has four special qualities. Firstly, when there's a disaster, it's a good choice for a warm meal. Victims can eat the rice without having to worry about safety and hygiene. Disaster relief workers also need good meals and rest, so the Jing Si Rice can provide nourishment and help them regain their strength."

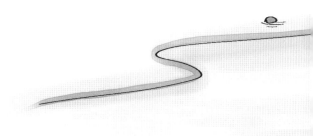

「香積飯的第二個特色，簡單、方便、省時。慈濟志工到現場賑災時，即使有準備食物，但大多是乾糧，此時若有熱水，直接沖泡香積飯，20分鐘後就有熱騰騰的蔬菜飯可以填飽肚子，沒有熱水時也可以用冷水沖泡，大約需要50到60分鐘之後，就可以吃了。緊急時，這就是一碗救命飯，同時也節省許多時間和人力、物力，十分環保。」

　　"Secondly, the Jing Si Instant Rice can be prepared easily, conveniently, and quickly. Tzu Chi volunteers usually bring food to the site of a disaster, but usually they only bring dried rations. But as long as they have hot water, they can prepare the instant rice in as little as 20 minutes, giving everyone a hot meal! When they don't have hot water, they can still use cold water to soak the rice, and it will be ready to eat in 50 to 60 minutes. This is a godsend during emergencies! This also helps save time and effort, and it's very environmentally friendly!"

「香積飯的第三個特色，非常時、方便法。以慈濟辦活動來說，香積志工準備用膳費時又費工，但是若以香積飯為底，再搭配其他簡單食物，準備時間縮短一半，所有志工都有機會聽經聞法，增加自我精進的機會，這才是最重要的。」

"Thirdly, the Jing Si Instant Rice saves a lot of time and effort. For example, when Tzu Chi holds an event, the volunteers preparing food used to have to spend a lot of time and effort cooking. But now if they use the Jing Si Instant Rice, they just need to prepare a few other simple dishes. This cuts their cooking time in half! Then the volunteers can also have a chance to hear the Dharma Masters speak, and this gives them a chance to improve their own cultivation!"

「香積飯的第四個特色，健康、好吃、省水電。現代家庭可以在家中準備香積飯，用餐時再加上幾道青菜，營養均衡，全家人在家一起享受用餐時刻。尤其夏天，煮飯的人一定也非常開心，用香積飯就不用煮飯煮到滿頭大汗。」

"And fourthly, the Jing Si Instant Rice is healthy and delicious while also reducing the use of electricity and water. Families can easily prepare the rice at home,

and then they just need to add some vegetable dishes for more balanced nutrition, and it's all done! They can enjoy a meal together! This is especially good in the summer, because the person doing the cooking won't need to do so much in the hot kitchen!"

「最後，請師父給我們一些鼓勵的話。」

「用開放的心面對自己、面對問題。剛來靜思精舍時，我連白飯都不會煮，現在居然成功研發香積飯！還有，身為弟子，『上人的心願在哪裡，弟子就要立願在哪裡』，這個信念也支持我，成就了香積飯的研發。」德晗師父謙虛的說。

"Dharma Master, can you give us some words of encouragement?"

"We should look at ourselves and look at our problems with an open mind. When I first came to the Jing Si Abode, I didn't even know how to cook rice! But now I've managed to develop the Jing Si Instant Rice!" Dharma Master De Han replied humbly. "Furthermore, as a disciple of Dharma Master Cheng Yen, I've learned that Dharma Master Cheng Yen's wishes should become my goals. This is the belief that drives me, and it led to the creation of the Jing Si Instant Rice."

「謝謝師父，我的採訪結束了，等我完成採訪稿，再分享給您。」

　　小願回家後，回想採訪的過程，她告訴自己，她也要像德晗師父一樣，用開放的心面對自己，用謙虛的態度面對挫折，以自己的力量，成就每一件美好的事物。

"Thank you, Dharma Master, that's all I needed to ask for my interview. I will share my report with you after I've finished it."

Xiao-Yuan thought back to her interview after she went home. She told herself that she should follow Dharma Master De Han's suggestion and look at herself with an open mind. She should also have a humble heart when she runs into setbacks, and should accomplish good things with her own abilities.

一起動手做做看
Let's try making it!

讀完好看的香積飯故事，現在讓我們一起動手做做看，完成好吃的香積飯和香積飯糰。

After learning about the story of the Jing Si Instant Rice, let's try making Jing Si Instant Rice and rice balls!

簡易好吃的香積飯食譜
Easy and delicious Jing Si Instant Rice Recipe

材料 Material

綜合蔬菜香積飯 1 份（淨斯香積飯系列產品：香醇咖哩、金黃甜玉米、義式番茄、海帶芽糙米等皆同作法。）

1 package of Garden Vegetables Jing Si Instant Rice (Other Jing Si Instant Rice flavors, including Curry, Sweet Corn, , Tomato Herb, and Seaweed are all cooked the same way)

作法 Instructions

1. 在碗中倒入約 120c.c. 熱開水。

1. Pour around 120c.c. of hot boiled water into a bowl.

2. 先倒入調味包，攪拌均勻使溶於水。

3. 再倒入蔬菜包和乾燥飯包，再次充分攪拌。

2. Add the flavor packet to the water and mix well.

3. Add the vegetable packet and dried rice to the water and mix well.

31

4. 讓米飯與蔬菜料都泡到熱
開水裡。

4. Make sure that the rice and vegetables are both covered
in water.

5. 蓋上碗蓋，靜置 20 分
鐘，打開攪拌後即可食用。

5. Cover the bowl and let
it sit 20 minutes, then
uncover it, mix well, and
serve.

6. 若不使用調味包及蔬菜包，以相同方式燜泡乾燥飯，即成一碗白飯。

6. If you do not add the flavor packet and vegetable packet, you can prepare just the rice in the same way to get a bowl of white rice.

小注釋：冷水也可以沖泡。

Note: You can use cold water too!

營養美味的香積飯糰食譜

Nutritious and delicious Jing Si Instant Rice Ball Recipe

材料 Material

海帶芽糙米香積飯 4 人份（含 4 小包乾燥飯、調味包、蔬菜包）		Seaweed Jing Si Instant Rice for 4 people (includes 4 packets of dried rice, flavor packets, and vegetable packets)
燕麥薏仁粉	4 湯匙	4 tablespoons of Oats and Job's Tears Instant Mix
蘿蔔乾	1 小碗	1 small bowl of dried radishes
乾香菇	3 朵	3 dried shiitake mushrooms
味噌	1 茶匙	1 teaspoon of miso
熱開水	480c.c.	480c.c. of hot boiled water

油少許、醬油少許、胡椒粉少許、黑芝麻少許

Oil, soy sauce, white pepper, and black sesame seeds to taste

作法 Instructions

1. 將 4 小包乾燥飯、2 包調味料（多寡依個人口味）倒入鍋中拌均。用熱開水沖泡後加蓋，燜 15 至 20 分鐘 （時間依個人對米飯的軟硬習慣）。

1. Add 4 packets of dried rice and 2 flavor packets (can be adjusted to taste) to a pot and mix well. Add the hot water, then cover and let it sit for 15 to 20 minutes (the time can be varied based on the preferred firmness of rice).

2. 蘿蔔乾和香菇切細，加少許油以中火爆香，再加少許醬油、胡椒粉，製成餡料。

2. Dice the dried radishes and shiitake mushrooms and sauté them in a small amount of oil. Add soy sauce and pepper. This will be the filling.

3. 將【作法1】料加入燕麥薏仁粉拌均後，取出放手掌壓平。在中間包入【作法2】的餡料，捏成三角形，兩面灑上黑芝蔴。

3. Add the Oats and Job's Tears Instant Mix to the mixture from Step 1 and mix well. Shape the mixture by hand into a

flat shape, then add the filling from Step 2. Shape the rice into a triangle and then sprinkle the sesame seeds on both sides.

4. 取 4 個碗。每個碗中放 1/4茶匙味噌，攪成液狀後， 倒入一包海帶芽蔬菜包，再 注入 120c.c. 開水，即成美 味素湯。

4. Take 4 bowls and add 1/4 teaspoon of miso to each bowl, and stir until it forms a liquid. Add 1 packet of seaweed to each bowl, and then add 120c.c. of hot boiled water to make miso soup.

靜思語：行願

願要大，志要堅，

氣要柔，心要細。

Our vows must be great, our commitment unwavering,
our temper gentle, and our mind attentive.

《靜思語第二集》｜《小學生 365 靜思語》

只要有心，

一定可以撥出時間；

只要有願，不怕沒有力量。

If we have the heart and will to do something,
we will be able to find the time and strength to do it.

《中英對照靜思小語 4》｜《小學生 365 靜思語》

天天發好願，時時做好事。

Do good deeds and make good wishes always every day.

《中英對照靜思小語 4》｜《小學生 365 靜思語》

有心就有福，有願就有力。

With good intentions come blessings.
With the will comes the strength.

《兒童靜思語中英對照 3》｜《小學生 365 靜思語》

心中有信，願力無窮；

心中無私，其福無量。

With faith, one will have unlimited willpower.
With selfless intentions, one will have boundless blessings.

《中英對照靜思小語 4》

關於香積飯

給老師和家長們更多關於香積飯的資訊。

照片為在海外賑災時，大家享用香積飯的情形。（攝影者：黃筱哲）

照片為師父們正在包裝香積飯。（攝影者：簡淑絲）

　　天搖地動、暴雨成災、一片殘破的災區，沒有電、沒有瓦斯，飢寒交迫，最直接需要的就是飲食。如何才能讓受困災區的鄉親能及時溫飽？證嚴上人想：「如果可將白米變成沖泡式的乾燥飯，用水浸泡，免烹煮就能即時有一碗飯或粥可以食用了。」上人對乾燥飯的期待，精舍師父聽到了。德晗師父與德偌師父，自 2006 年開始實驗，終於在眾緣合和之下，用冷水或熱水浸泡，免烹煮就可以食用的「香積飯」問世。「香」是芬芳馥馨，「積」是因緣積聚 ─ 保存食物的原味，傳遞人情的溫暖。來自於鄉土，純淨無染之香甜御米，香積飯的研發是為國際賑災或急難救助使用，節能方便、自然環保，當應用在急難救災時，不僅快速方便，有水就可用餐。若能推展到家家戶戶使用，每天早上無須買早餐，只要有熱開水沖泡，即能吃到有蔬菜的飯食，既省水又省電。

　　走訪「靜思書軒」就可以深入了解各種口味的香積飯喔！

靜思人文
JING SI CULTURE

靜思精舍惜物造福的智慧故事 2

行願：香積飯的故事

總 策 劃／靜思書軒
編 　審／釋德晗
照片提供／慈濟基金會文史處
故 　事／陳佳聖
插 　圖／江長芳
美術設計／羅吟軒
英 　譯／Linguitronics Co., Ltd. 萬象翻譯（股）公司（故事及主題延伸）

總 編 輯／李復民
副總編輯／鄧懿貞
特約主編／陳佳聖
封面設計／Javick 工作室
專案企劃／蔡孟庭、盤惟心

讀書共和國出版集團 業務平台

總 經 理／李雪麗　　　　　　副總經理／李復民
海外業務總監／張鑫峰　　　　特販業務總監／陳綺瑩
零售資深經理／郭文弘　　　　專案企劃總監／蔡孟庭
印務協理／江域平　　　　　　印務主任／李孟儒

出 　版／發光體文化・遠足文化事業股份有限公司
發 　行／遠足文化事業股份有限公司（讀書共和國出版集團）
地 　址／231 新北市新店區民權路 108 之 2 號 9 樓
電 　話／(02) 2218-1417　　　傳真／(02) 8667-1065
電子信箱／service@bookrep.com.tw
網 　址／www.bookrep.com.tw
郵撥帳號／19504465 遠足文化事業股份有限公司

法律顧問／華洋法律事務所　蘇文生律師
印 　製／凱林彩印股份有限公司

慈濟人文出版社
地 　址／臺北市忠孝東路三段二一七巷七弄十九號一樓
電 　話／(02) 2898-9888
傳 　真／(02) 2898-9889
網 　址／www.jingsi.org

2024 年 5 月 2 日初版一刷　　　定價／320 元
ISBN ／ 978-626-98109-7-0（精裝）　書號／2IGN1006

國家圖書館出版品預行編目 (CIP) 資料

靜思精舍惜物造福的智慧故事 . 2, 行願 : 香積飯的故事 =
The wisdom of cherishing and sowing blessings at the
Jing Si Abode. 2, vow to action : the story of rice ／ 陳佳
聖故事 . -- 初版 . -- 新北市 : 遠足文化事業股份有限公司發
光體文化 , 遠足文化事業股份有限公司 , 2024.04
　面；　公分
中英對照
ISBN 978-626-98109-7-0(精裝)

224.515　　　　　　　　　　　　113003672